thepeople

theart

thetalk

KU-005-605

Street art is art that is specially designed for the streets. It can be funny, surprising and entertaining, and often makes people think more carefully about the streets they walk down. Street artists create sculptures, 3D designs and can even turn themselves into art, with mime artists, flash mobs and living statues giving performances to passers-by.

STREET STYLE!

Art for every environment!

Street artists use many different styles and locations to produce their work. For example, they might alter disused road signs to create something unique, or use random, everyday objects (such as chewing gum stuck to a pavement!) to create colourful, eye-catching designs. That really is art on the street!

Taking it to the streets

Some artists might make their art in a studio, then put it in a public place where they think it will have the most impact. Streetsmart, quirky and forever changing, street art can be anything the artist wants it to be. Go ahead and explore – the street is your canvas!

Turning junk into art!

Street artists can turn anything and everything into art. They can paint designs on cardboard boxes or make sculptures out of old plastic cups or dustbin liners. The recycled nature of street art can help make the art cheap to create, but it also makes a point to governments about waste, and how people throw away too many things.

a Mirko Flodin
tyre beast sculpture

Mark Jenkins' 'disappearing
head' body cast

CRAZY SCULPTURES

Type 'Mark Jenkins street' into
www.youtube.com to see the
double takes of passers-by!

a fibreglass
cow sculpture

Sculptures date back thousands of years and are traditionally carved from expensive, hard-to-find materials, such as marble or bronze. Street art sculptures are different – they are made out of whatever the artist wants to use to create the biggest impact!

Tyres turn into art

German sculptor Mirko Flodin turns recycled tyres into great street art. His sculptures of horses, dragons, sharks and other extraordinary beasts have been shown across Europe and the Far East.

The packing tape king

Mark Jenkins, an American street artist, makes installations out of transparent packing tape. Mark has been known to cover parking meters with tape to make big lollipop 'heads', and to take casts of his own body and leave them in surprising places around the city streets. One famous sculpture looks like a man's head has disappeared into the building he is leaning against!

Galleries on the street

Imaginative street artists around the world are creating unusual sculptures such as the fibreglass cows that were part of a travelling exhibition called Cow Parade in 2006, featuring hundreds of eye-catching cow sculptures!

Dogs bite back

Simple DIY dog sculptures first started appearing in public areas in Sweden in 2006, and have since spread around the world. Made from wood, plastic and fabric, this form of street art began as an expression of rebellion against expensive art commissioned by the government.

GOING GLOBAL

From Montmartre, Paris, to Melbourne, Australia, street artists are hard at work creating something new. Their work is bright, bold and out in the open. Here are some of the highlights.

Johannesburg, South Africa

Mary Sibande's series of street art images appeared around the city on billboards and the sides of buildings in 2010. Mary creates fibreglass casts of her own body, which she paints black and dresses in colourful Victorian-style costumes. She then photographs the results to create striking, powerful images of life-like dolls.

Mary Sibande's dolls are dressed in elaborate costumes (left). People often feature in Swoon's art (above).

New York, USA

Swoon is one of the world's most famous female street artists. She specialises in life-size wheatpaste prints and paper cut-outs that are stuck to walls and brighten up the city. Her work can also be seen in galleries such as The Museum of Modern Art, New York.

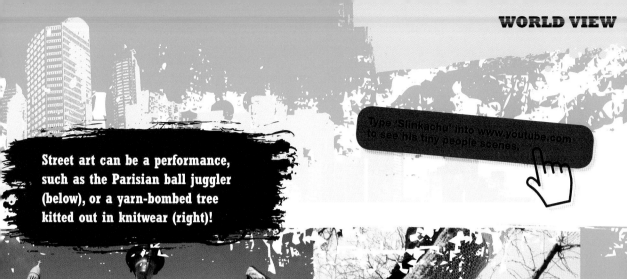

Street art can be a performance, such as the Parisian ball juggler (below), or a yarn-bombed tree kitted out in knitwear (right)!

Type 'Slinkachu' into www.youtube.com to see his tiny people scenes.

London, England

Street artist, photographer and blogger, Slinkachu, creates life-like street scenes using miniature railway figures as models. His photographs show couples living on tennis ball desert islands or rowing boats in puddles of spilt milk!

Montmartre, Paris

The traditional home of great French artists, including Toulouse-Lautrec, this district in Paris is now home to street entertainers such as the unique ball juggler who performs acrobatic tricks!

Melbourne, Australia

This south Australian city has one of the most active street art scenes in the world. Since 2004, it has hosted an annual ten-day Stencil Festival, which has featured more than 800 works from 150 artists, as well as live demonstrations, artist talks and workshops.

Stockholm, Sweden

Founded in Paris in 2006, the Swedish yarn-bombing collective 'Masquerade' turn their environment into a colourful, knitted playground. They cover statues, lampposts and concrete bollards. They even decorated the streets with knitted flowers! Their work can be seen around the world, from Finland to Russia and Iceland, as well as at home in Sweden.

THE TARZAN

German street artist Johan Lorbeer created 'the Tarzan', an attention-grabbing performance piece that amazes audiences across Europe. Johan hangs above a crowd, seemingly stuck to the wall with his bare hand! But how does he do it?

Essential technique

- Good head for heights
- Upper body strength
- Plenty of stamina
- Ability to stay still for long periods of time

Type 'Johan Lorbeer Tarzan' into www.youtube.com to watch Johan at work.

HOW IT'S DONE

1. The arm that is leaning against the wall is a fake arm.

2. The fake arm – strong enough to hold Johan's weight – is part of a metal frame. One end of the frame is attached to the wall, the rest is hidden inside Johan's clothes, running down his back and attached to his shoes so that his weight is evenly distributed.

3. Johan is raised onto a building, and the fake arm and frame are attached to the wall. Because of the height, passers-by cannot see the frame, or the fact that the arm is not real!

Why do it?

The Tarzan is one of Johan's most famous performances. He 'hangs' in the air for hours on end, barely moving or speaking. He looks almost like a statue, and the longer he goes without speaking, the more interested the crowd becomes. Johan has created a unique and memorable form of street art!

HOT AIR ARTIST

My story by Joshua Allen Harris

As a child, I loved drawing and painting but never thought I could do it for a living. After I left school, I spent ten years working in retail, but always regretted not pursuing art, so in 2005, I decided to go back to college to study.

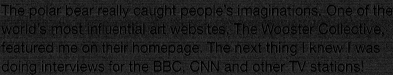

When I was at college, I was fascinated by the street art I saw in New York and decided that I also wanted to create something out in the open for the public to see. One day, I saw a carrier bag blowing in the wind and it gave me an idea. At the time, there was a lot of talk of global warming and how the ice caps were melting. I decided to create a polar bear 'sculpture' – using packing tape and carrier bags – and attached it to the subway grate. Whenever a train went by underground, the warm air would rise and bring the bear to life. When the train had passed, the bear 'died' again.

The polar bear really caught people's imaginations. One of the world's most influential art websites, The Wooster Collective, featured me on their homepage. The next thing I knew I was doing interviews for the BBC, CNN and other TV stations!

After the polar bear, I experimented with different animals, from a sea monster to a gorilla. Crowds of strangers would gather, waiting for the next train to go by so the sculptures would 'come to life'. My work has brought people together – it's been a wonderful experience.

Type 'air bear' into www.youtube.com to see the polar bear in action!

LEON REID IV

Street art pioneer

THE STATS

Name: Leon Reid IV
Also known as: VERBS, Darius Jones
Born: 18 September 1979
Place of birth: Richmond, Virginia
Job: Street artist

Growing up with graffiti

Leon started out as a graffiti artist at the age of 15, using the street name VERBS. Leon's family had left his hometown of Richmond to move to Cincinnati, Ohio. 'Street-bombing' – covering buildings with graffiti – was all the rage, and Leon and his friends would leave their tags all over the city.

The streets of New York

In 1998, the young artist moved to New York to study at the Pratt Institute, one of America's most influential art schools. He dropped the name VERBS and began working as Darius Jones, progressing from spray-can art to 3D street art. There, he met film students Quenell Jones and Brad Downey, and the three men became a street art trio. They disguised themselves as construction workers with hard hats and reflective vests, and travelled the city bending, welding and reworking everyday objects, such as road signs and telephone boxes. Between them, they created around 150 amazing street art sculptures.

Heading to London

Next stop was London, where Leon studied for a master's degree in fine art from 2003 to 2004. He kept producing his street sculptures. He enjoyed playing with road signs – one of his most famous pieces shows a silhouetted 'man' catching his wife and child as they 'fall off' a Children Crossing sign. He also added a fake zebra crossing pole next to an existing one to make the two poles look like they were kissing.

Turning street art into money

Leon returned to the USA in 2005, and started working almost exclusively on projects that were commissioned by city councils, art festivals and private companies. He now has the budget, the time and the access to create street art that everyone can enjoy! Leon is recognised around the world as a truly original and innovative street artist.

career highlights

2003 created 'Hent Glacier', a steel rose that sprouted from the New York pavement.

2004 created 'The Kiss' to London – two zebra crossing signs that appear to be kissing.

2008 published 'The Adventures of Darius and Downey'.

2009 produced 'True Yank', a sculpture of President Lincoln for Urbis Gallery, Manchester.

Leon's 'True Yank' sculpture shows President Lincoln wearing a baseball cap and hip-hop jewellery.

GUERRILLA ART

Street art comes in all shapes and sizes! It's all about making an impact and spreading the message of art in the urban environment...

art on the street by Adam Neate

Cardboard city

Adam Neate started painting on cardboard boxes left in the street because he could not afford canvases. Now one of the most famous UK street artists, Adam estimates he has left 5,000 works around London – and once left out 1,000 box designs in one night!

Guerrilla gardening

Who says street art has to be limited to the concrete? Artists are using cities' green spaces, too, planting vegetable patches on scruffy roundabouts that form eye-catching shapes, or surprisingly colourful flower beds in missing pavement slabs. Guerrilla gardening brings colour and life to urban environments.

Knitting graffiti

A group of street artists from Texas, USA, began the 'knit graffiti' or 'yarn-bombing' craze in 2005. Artists wrap lampposts, parking meters and street signs with colourful knits and crochets to make street art a little more cosy! Groups have since sprung up worldwide, from New York and Sydney to Milan and Mexico City.

guerrilla gardening in Ghent, Belgium

crocheted by yarn-bombers!

Type 'Madison yarn-bombing' into www.youtube.com to see an amazing yarn-bombing project.

MYLZ

Type 'Julian Beever art' into www.youtube.com to see some of Julian's amazing creations!

Radar expert, Mylz, is a street artist, DJ and director of Hedz Ltd, a creative arts and design organisation that works with young people from all backgrounds. Here, he tells Radar what street art is and why it is his favourite art form.

Did you enjoy art at school?

Actually, I found it quite boring! I used to choose my own subjects to draw – cartoons or my favourite album covers – and then hand them in as coursework. They would get marked, so I guess my teacher could tell that I was inspired, even if it wasn't by his lessons!

What is your definition of street art?

It is any artwork that reflects contemporary urban lifestyle and culture. Artists can choose to work in any form or with any materials that they feel reflects them best.

How can you train to become a street artist?

Well, there are no street art training courses! My advice would be to work out what types of street art you are interested in, find out who are the best artists producing these styles, study their work and create your own versions. Try not to copy other artists directly, but don't worry about taking influences – this is how many street artists develop their styles.

How can I start creating street art?

If you want to be good, you need lots of practice, which you can't do in a hurry on the street. A cheap plank of wood can be a good starting point. Prime it with emulsion, and then paint over it. Once you've done some artwork that you're happy with, mount it on your bedroom wall!

Who are the most exciting street artists working today?

Chu, Julian Beever and N4T4 are all breaking new ground and expanding people's opinions and expectations.

What makes a great piece of street art?

A good idea and a clean, careful execution are all you need. The location can give a piece even more impact. If you create a work of art that totally transforms a boring or dull environment, it will really stand out!

Where are the best places in the world to see street art?

Barcelona, Spain, used to be a hotspot but recently a lot of the art there has been removed. Bristol and Birmingham in the UK are very up-and-coming, and areas of London and New York are really impressive. As street art gains more of a positive reputation, hopefully the artwork will gain respect, and artistic areas within cities will be preserved.

ART IS THE WORD

Know your 'tags' from your 'buffs', and learn to speak the language of street art with Radar's handy guide!

3D art
three-dimensional letters and images

bronze
a yellowish-brown mixture of copper and tin that is used to make sculptures

buff
to remove or cover over a piece of street art

burn
to 'outdo' another artist's work or achievements

canvases
pieces of canvas fabric that have been stretched and prepared for artists to work on

cast
a kind of hollow sculpture – in the shape of a human body, for example

empty show
an exhibition held in a derelict building

emulsion
a type of paint with a matt effect

fibreglass
a light, strong material popular with street artists that is made from fine glass fibres

flash mob
a group of people who gather suddenly in a public place, perform an unusual piece of art, and then leave

getting up
going out to make art

guerrilla art
art created by a small organised group, sometimes politically motivated, working outside of the normal rules and regulations of society

installation
an artwork created when artists use 3D objects and space

living statue
a mime artist who poses like a statue, sometimes for hours on end

marble
hard rock, often used for carving sculptures

Humour meets street sculpture as a 'workman' surfaces from a manhole!

Street sculpture meets graffiti art! This cow street sculpture features a mural too.

mural
an image that is painted directly onto a wall

street bombing
covering buildings with graffiti

wheatpaste
homemade glue used for putting up posters

roller
a large art piece often done on canvas that hangs down from a rooftop. It is painted with a paint roller on a pole

tag
a graffiti artist's basic style of signature, a little like their own logo

yarn-bombing
covering street furniture, such as lampposts and railings, with knitting

GLOSSARY

carve
to cut or chip into a hard object to create a new shape

class divide
the separation between rich, often educated people and poor, often uneducated people

commissioned
to be asked to create a piece of art on behalf of another person or organisation

crochet
to make something, usually out of wool, by looping and weaving thread with a hooked needle

disposable
made of cheap materials; designed to be thrown away, rather than kept

disused
thrown away, neglected or not used

DIY
stands for 'do it yourself'. Something that is done at home rather than by professionals

endurance
to do something for a long period of time

illusion
a false or misleading appearance; a deceptive view of reality

influential
someone or something in a position of importance

innovative
full of ideas; introducing new styles or new ways of doing something

peripheral vision
something that you see 'out of the corner of your eye' rather than looking straight at it

prime
to apply a primer or layer of special paint to prepare wood for painting

subculture
a small part of mainstream culture, with its own attitudes, beliefs and influences

Tarot cards
special cards with distinctive symbols used for telling people's fortunes

DAVID BLAINE

THE STATS

Name: David Blaine White
Born: 4 April 1973
Place of birth: Brooklyn, New York
Nationality: American
Job: Street artist, magician, endurance artist

The young illusionist

David Blaine became fascinated with cards and illusions by watching his grandmother give Tarot card readings. He picked up a deck of playing cards when he was five years old, and says he has been practising ever since. At a young age, David also developed an early taste for risking life and limb, and still has a scar on the bridge of his nose where an attempted backflip off a park bench went wrong!

Suffering for art

More recently, David has moved towards his own form of installation street art – blending illusion and performance with a series of endurance feats, watched by audiences around the world. His 'Frozen In Time' stunt in 2000 required him to be encased in a block of ice for nearly 64 hours in the middle of Times Square, New York. For 'Vertigo' in 2002, David stood on top of a 30-metre pillar for 35 hours! For his 'Drowned Alive' feat in New York in 2006 (pictured here), David immersed himself in a giant sphere of water for one week.

Magic man

After leaving home at 17, David supported himself in New York by performing magic tricks at private parties. He then moved to the South of France, where he performed at the mansions of millionaires. These days, David can still make around US $100,000 (£63,000) per night for a private show! In 1997, his first television special *David Blaine: Street Magic* was broadcast. The young performer focused more on the audience's reaction to his tricks, and adapted them in response. This added an exciting new element to a traditional form of entertainment.

What's next?

David is a master of holding his breath, and broke the world record live on television in 2008 when he held his breath for 17 minutes and 4.4 seconds on *The Oprah Winfrey Show*. David is always searching for the next great show-stopping piece of street art performance. So, what is he planning next? Well, he is said to be fascinated by people who jump off Niagara Falls in the USA and survive! With his constant drive to entertain, and his willingness to attempt never-seen-before acts of skill and endurance, David is the most exciting, and the most famous, street performer in the world!

STREET STATS!

1:87

3

The scale of the model people in artist Slinkachu's work. In other words, $\frac{1}{87}$th of their real size.

The number of hours it took street artist Joshua Allen Harris to create his 'sea monster' sculpture from plastic bags.

WHAT ARE YOU LOOKING AT?

2004

1 MILLION

The year that the term 'flash mob' was added to the Oxford English Dictionary.

The estimated value of artworks in pounds sterling distributed in one night on London streets by Adam Neate on 14 November 2008.

1,000

Estimated number of legal street artworks on view in Melbourne, Australia.

40

The number of cities around the world taking part in the flash-mob event, International Pillow Fight Day 2011.

3,822

The number of minutes David Blaine was encased in ice in New York's Time Square for his stunt 'Frozen in Time'.

1973

The year guerrilla gardening began in New York.

THE FLASH MOB

In the age of instant communication via the internet and mobile phones, a surreal form of street performance has emerged. This street style is called the flash mob, and it's coming to a town near you!

The birth of the flash mob

Journalist Bill Wasik claims to have created the flash mob movement in 2003. Co-ordinating four groups in separate New York bars, he arranged for more than 100 people to meet in the rug department of the famous Macy's store. The crowd all claimed to be flatmates, who were shopping for a new rug, and always made their buying decisions together! Bill's next 'performances' were a 15-second spontaneous round of applause in a hotel lobby, and an invasion of a shoe shop by a group claiming to be foreign tourists!

The art of dancing

Flash mobs have caught on around the world in a variety of entertaining ways. London has played host to a number of 'silent discos' where a crowd gathers at a set time and begins dancing to music it can hear through wireless headphones. In April 2007, one silent disco at London's Victoria Station attracted more than 4,000 participants!

Fighting with feathers

One of the most successful and long-running flash mobs is International Pillow Fight Day. The first event took place in March 2008, with more than 25 cities around the world participating. In New York, more than 5,000 people attended, making it the largest flash mob ever recorded. The event for 2011 took place in cities from Toronto to Paris and Melbourne to Istanbul. Organiser Kevin Bracken thinks the phenomenon is showing no signs of stopping. 'We hope [International Pillow Fight Day] will become a large part of popular culture. Now the internet has enabled it, there is no reason for these events not to happen forever!'

Flash mobbing got scary in 2009 when zombie mobbers hit Warsaw city in Poland (above and left)!

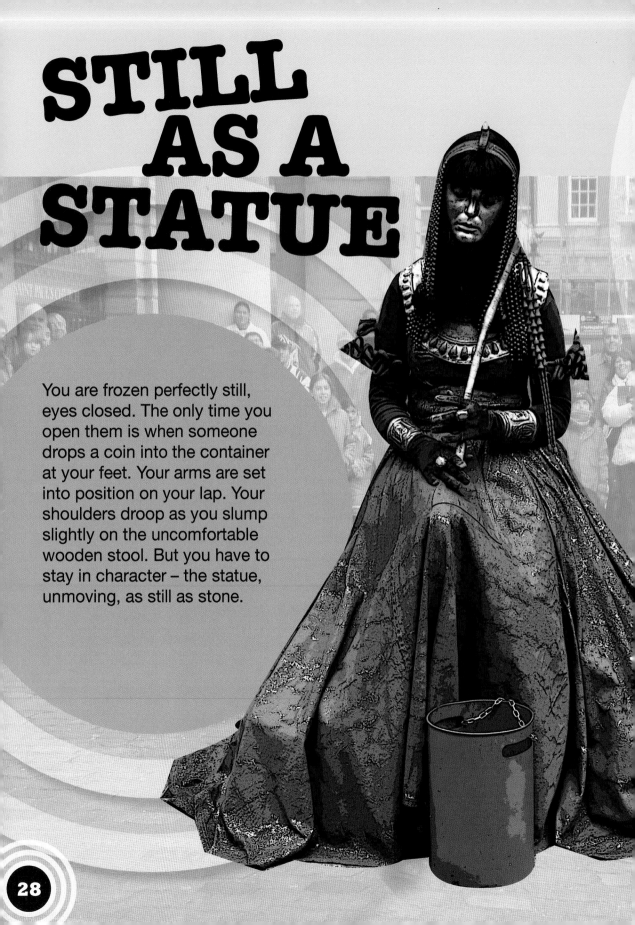

STILL AS A STATUE

You are frozen perfectly still, eyes closed. The only time you open them is when someone drops a coin into the container at your feet. Your arms are set into position on your lap. Your shoulders droop as you slump slightly on the uncomfortable wooden stool. But you have to stay in character – the statue, unmoving, as still as stone.

Get prepared!

You have worked on your outfit for weeks, painting and shading the dress, accessories and shoes to look just right. Now it's finished, it's like your masterpiece. You decided to paint your face and hands this morning on the street – you didn't want to get on the train in the full costume! Your face paint is as thick as mud, itchy and uncomfortable. You are pleased it's not a hot day – that would be unbearable!

Time for action

A small, curious crowd has gathered: a few tourists, and some mothers with small children. It's amazing what you can sense, even with your eyes closed! You cannot make the smallest movement. The children's eyes are as big as saucers as they watch you. Then a little girl drops a coin into your pot. Slowly, you come to life. You must climb off your chair and bow in thanks to her. There are laughs and a little applause from the crowd as you slowly climb back onto your stool.

Feeling the strain

The day has been a success, but your shoulders ache from holding your arms in one place and the effort of keeping them so still. As the final shopper leaves the street, you leave your seat. Your joints creak like old doors, glad of the movement. You look forward to the journey home. The life of a statue – it is harder than people think.

ART FOR ALL?

Street art fans love it for its free expression, and the way it brings city streets to life. They say that:

1. Street art allows everyone to express themselves, whether rich or poor. People can start by painting on cardboard boxes or scraps of wood if they cannot afford other materials.

2. Street artists make people look at and appreciate the urban environment in a whole new way.

3. Artists such as Leon Reid IV and Slinkachu have put street art on the map. They have attracted a lot of new fans who want to be part of a cool, mysterious, underground subculture.

4. Environmentally friendly and using all kinds of disused materials, street art is the ultimate in recycling!

5. There is no class divide and no snobbery with street art. It is not hidden away in art galleries, it is out in the open for everyone to see and enjoy.

6. Street artists are in touch with their audience and have a better idea of what interests them than traditional artists.

7. Now a regular feature in art galleries, street art can be regarded as just as important and well-respected as traditional art.

However, some people think that street art is antisocial, and is spoiling our environment. They say that:

1. Street art that is created without the permission of a city council or property owner is illegal and no better than vandalism.

2. Thousands of pounds worth of damage to buildings and street signs can be caused by street artists who do not respect public property.

3. Artists trying to create new, unexpected pieces of street art might take unnecessary risks and injure themselves.

4. Crowds gathering to look at street art or to take part in flash mobs can cause obstructions in busy pedestrian areas, shops and hotels. Police time will be wasted by supervising these gatherings when they could be out catching criminals.

AGAINST

Right or wrong?

Street art can bring city streets to life and is a great way for people to express themselves. Making sculptures out of packing tape, or creating disposable artwork on cardboard is imaginative and harms no-one. As long as street artists respect other people's property and do not damage it, street art can be enjoyed and supported by everyone.

ART ATTACK!

People to talk to

Street art is exciting, creative and open to everyone. You can use just about anything to make it and you don't need a gallery to display your creations – let the street showcase these masterpieces!

Hedz
To find out all about street art from Radar's own expert, Mylz, contact Hedz, the creative arts and design organisation: **www.hedz.ltd.uk**

Street art online

You can enjoy some fantastic street art from around the world by going to: **www.woostercollective.com**

Check out this eye-popping collection of street artists: **www.thelondonpolice.com**

Watch street art

Type 'Mark Jenkins street art installations' into www.youtube.com to see some video of some of his extraordinary work.

Type '3D street art the crevasse' into www.youtube.com to see the creation of a stunning piece of street art.

Reads & Apps

Street Art Cookbook: A Guide To Techniques and Materials by Benke Carlsson (Dokument Press, 2010)

Urban Interventions: Personal Projects in Public Places by Robert Klanten (Die Gestalten Verlag, 2010)

For apps with art head to iTunes for *Street Art Magazine* and *BStyle*: **www.itunes.com**

INDEX